Original title:
Life, Laughter, and Lost Keys

Copyright © 2025 Creative Arts Management OÜ
All rights reserved.

Author: Isaac Ravenscroft
ISBN HARDBACK: 978-1-80566-193-1
ISBN PAPERBACK: 978-1-80566-488-8

Smiles in Unexpected Places

A cat in a hat, sells shoes by the road,
With socks on his paws, he lightens the load.
A bird on a swing, sings silly old tunes,
While clouds drift above, like whimsical loons.

A sandwich with legs, runs off with a pickle,
Chasing after fries, oh what a tricky fickle!
Giggling through corners, where socks tend to hide,
The laughter of echoes, where memories bide.

Enigmas of the Heartbeat

You trip on a shoe, that was left by a clown,
It bounces and laughs, as you tumble down.
The rhythm of giggles, in a heart that does race,
With every odd moment, a surprising embrace.

A tickle from fate, as you search for your key,
In a pocket of wonders, where nothing should be.
The dance of a drum, plays a random old song,
While secrets keep swirling, where nothing feels wrong.

The Conundrum of Crumpled Notes

A crumpled-up paper, whispers 'you forgot',
In a dance with the breeze, in a carefree plot.
An arrow of laughter, points straight at the sun,
With riddles of giggles, that have just begun.

A map drawn in crayon, leads nowhere at best,
Where giggles are treasures, that never do rest.
Each wrinkle a story, that teeters on chance,
In the chaos of moments, we find our own dance.

Mischievous Echoes in Hallways

Footsteps that prance, on a long winding stair,
A ghost wearing glasses, with quite the wild flair.
They squeak and they snicker, as shadows play peek,
Through hallways of humor, where whispers can speak.

A door that won't open, and yet swings with glee,
While giggles are trapped, in the space 'tween the key.
The funny reflections, in corners unplanned,
Make every dull moment, astonishingly grand.

The Pursuit of Whimsy Through Stolen Glances

In the park where shadows dance,
Laughter skips, as toes advance.
Chasing dreams on a flying kite,
Each twist and turn, a laughing fright.

A cat in a hat grins with glee,
While squirrels plot to steal the tea.
Under a tree, a joke takes flight,
Our chuckles echo into the night.

Echoes of Joy Beneath the Staircase

Under steps where secrets lie,
Whispers bounce as time goes by.
A sock, a shoe, a riddle sings,
Where laughter erupts, joy takes wing.

The creaks and groans begin to tease,
Silent chuckles drift in the breeze.
Tangled thoughts on every stick,
Unraveling smiles with every trick.

The Treasure Chest of Radiant Memories

In a box where treasures gleam,
Forgotten smiles, a golden dream.
A crumpled note, a toy's embrace,
Each piece a memory, time's soft grace.

A rubber duck sings a silly tune,
While shadows dance beneath the moon.
Laughter prickles the edges of night,
In every keepsake, pure delight.

Clues in the Constellation of Cheer

Stars above in playful rows,
Whispers of joy, the way it flows.
A puzzle brave on a starlit path,
Guides through giggles and aftermath.

A bumblebee dons a tiny hat,
Buzzing secrets, how about that?
With each whimsical step we take,
The universe chuckles, no mistake.

Dances with Destinies Unlocked

In a world where doors can't be found,
The jester twirls, feet off the ground.
With each misplaced key in a sock,
He giggles once, then gives a knock.

The moon winks down like a cheeky friend,
As the clock ticks on, we laugh, suspend.
Chasing the shadows of what we lose,
Reveling in mischief, hearts let loose.

Whirlwinds of Forgotten Glee

Around we go in circles bright,
As giggles soar like kites in flight.
A salad of moments, tossed in time,
With bites of joy, they seem to rhyme.

Step on the toes of that absent tune,
Twist in a whirl, like a wild cartoon.
Lost in our dance, we're not alone,
The key to happiness? A giggle blown.

Lock and Laughter: A Playful Pairing

Keys jangled loud, a raucous sound,
As giggles echo all around.
A cupboard jokes, 'I'm not the one!'
While we seek out what's lost in fun.

With every chuckle, doors come ajar,
Unlocking memories, near and far.
So let's embrace the silly muck,
In a world where the locked just never stuck.

The Hidden Joy of Lost Paths

In tangled streets where no one knows,
We stumble on where laughter grows.
With every route that seems askew,
A treasure waits in every view.

The spiteful keys dance in the mist,
While unseen joys make life persist.
Wander we will, through mishaps bold,
Creating tales that never get old.

The Harmony of Unhinged Laughter

In a world where jokes collide,
Tickles and giggles do abide.
A banana peel creates a scene,
Tripping on humor, just routine.

When clowns forget their big red nose,
Unexpected chaos surely flows.
Confetti rains from a secret stash,
A party begins with a silly splash.

Joy and jest weave through the air,
With pratfalls that create a flair.
Each chuckle springs from the absurd,
In harmony, not a single word.

A jester juggles thoughts unchained,
In playful antics, none are pained.
Life's a laugh and never bland,
Embrace the fun with open hands.

Finding Whimsy in the Mundane

A sock escapes the laundry dread,
It dances off, with dreams instead.
The toaster pops in a comical way,
   Breakfast turns to a funny play.

An umbrella flips in a gusty breeze,
   It flails around like it's at ease.
   A cat gets tangled in its own tail,
In simple moments, laughter prevails.

A spilled drink leads to a splash fight,
With bubbly giggles, oh what a sight!
Each tiny mishap, a chance to grin,
   In every corner, humor spins.

The mundane winks with a playful gaze,
   Finding joy in the simplest ways.
   When the ordinary starts to gleam,
   Laughter bubbles up like a dream.

The Charm of the Mislaid

In pockets deep, the treasures hide,
Where minutes are lost and chaos tried.
A charm bracelet left on the bus,
Turns everyday woes to a fuss.

Keys go missing like socks do,
In the fridge or stuck in a shoe.
A puzzle box marks the location,
With laughter, not frustration's sensation.

They turn up in the oddest spots,
Hey! There's a shoehorn and some knots!
Each misplace tells a funny tale,
A whimsied life with laughs that sail.

So next time things run off from sight,
Recall the joy, embrace the light.
For in the search for missing things,
Laughter reigns like bird on wing.

Laughter in the Wake of Chaos

When the world spins out of control,
A giggle erupts, a funny hole.
Spilled cereal becomes a dance,
As chaos leads to a silly chance.

Midst tangled cords and lost remote,
We find ourselves in a funny boat.
The dog steals the sandwich, oh dear me,
Turns dinner into comedy.

A slip on a rug sparks a roar,
Echoing laughter from ceiling to floor.
In mess and mayhem, joy is found,
In every moment, laughter abounds.

With chaos swirling like a breeze,
We laugh and dodge with playful ease.
In the wake of the wildest ride,
Humor smirks, cannot be denied.

A Symphony of Giggles Past

In a room filled with cheer,
Echoes of laughter near.
Once, we danced with no care,
Now we search everywhere.

The tickle of a funny thought,
Like a bubble, it can't be caught.
We waltzed on slipper floors,
And opened imaginary doors.

We whispered secrets in the night,
Each giggle a tiny flight.
With shadows that grew so tall,
We played until the night did fall.

The clock ticks on, but we sing,
Every moment is a new fling.
Though things may have slipped away,
The joy lives on in bright display.

Chasing Shadows with a Smile

We chase the shadows under the sun,
With silly hats, we have our fun.
In this game of peek and hide,
We find our joy, can't be denied.

Each chuckle is a fleeting breeze,
A moment of joy that's sure to tease.
Through puddles we splash, forgetting the fuss,
As the world spins round for all of us.

What's lost in pockets, found in jest,
A missing sock or a quirky fest.
With every snort and giggling spark,
We brighten up the evening dark.

So here we are, in the grand parade,
With shadows laughing, never to fade.
The joy we share is quite a thrill,
As we chase the sun, and time stands still.

The Riddle of the Rusty Lock

A rusty lock upon the shelf,
Holds secrets of a roguish elf.
With a jiggle and a twist,
Unlocking joy that can't be missed.

Each key we find is a tale untold,
Of mischief made when we were bold.
With each wrong turn, a chuckle high,
As memories dance like clouds in the sky.

What treasures hide behind this gate?
A pet rock, or a silly fate?
We spin the old tales, twist and twirl,
And giggles unfurl like a precious pearl.

So join the quest, let's laugh and see,
What curious wonders there might be.
A riddle here, a giggle there,
In this whimsical life, we share.

When Memories Are Just a Turn Away

A dusty path leads to our past,
With whispered secrets held steadfast.
Each corner turned brings a grin,
Where mischief waits and tales begin.

We spin around the stories told,
Of sticky fingers and dreams of gold.
With every giggle, we rewind time,
In playful moments, we lose the climb.

Keys that jingle in the breeze,
Unlocking laughter with silly ease.
Though moments fade like shadows cast,
The joy we forged is built to last.

So let's embrace this curious game,
Where all that's lost is never the same.
With every turn, let's celebrate,
The funny tales we cultivate.

The Hidden Keys to Unwritten Stories

In pockets deep, where treasures hide,
A jingle here, a riddle tied.
Unlock the tales, both strange and sweet,
With keyless wishes, life's a treat.

In every twist, a chance to laugh,
A mislaid path, a crooked half.
Giggles echo in forgotten halls,
For joy is found where memory calls.

Unraveled Threads of Blissful Chaos

Tangled yarn tossed in the air,
A playful mess beyond compare.
Each knot a giggle, each tangle a cheer,
In chaos lies a vibrant sphere.

Between the stitches of daydreamed schemes,
Bright colors burst in wildest themes.
With every twist, a merry chase,
In every stumble, a smiling face.

Giggles in the Attic of Time

Dusty boxes with treasures piled,
Whispers of laughter from every child.
Forgotten hats and shoes askew,
In the attic, joy is overdue.

Tick-tock echoes from the old clock's face,
Remind us all to embrace the chase.
Between each tick, a chuckle gleams,
In stolen moments, we weave our dreams.

A Map of Merriment and Wayward Paths

Drawn with crayons on a napkin wide,
Paths of folly where laughter lied.
X marks the spot for a sloshed-up grin,
Every turn leads you back again.

With each step taken, a joke unfolds,
In silly tales, our courage bolds.
So follow the signs with whimsical cheer,
For happiness blooms when the road's unclear.

Wanderlust of Abandoned Keys

Once a key danced with a door,
Craving adventures, wanting more.
But alas, it took a wrong turn,
Now it's lost, a lesson to learn.

It dreams of locks from far-off lands,
With treasures waiting in strange hands.
Yet all it has is a rusty ring,
And no more songs for it to sing.

In pockets deep or under beds,
It wonders where it could have led.
A journey cut short, a fate unkind,
With memories scatterbrained in its mind.

What stories could it tell if found?
Of laughter, mischief, and joy profound.
But here it sits, all stuck and blue,
A lonely key, still searching, too.

Half-Forgotten Tales of Fun

In a chest, old stories hide,
Of moments lost and time's wild ride.
A raucous laugh, a playful jest,
Tucked in corners where shadows rest.

A tale of socks that went askew,
And spoons that danced 'till morning's dew.
Puppets that traveled on wild quests,
To entertain the lively guests.

Once, a mop wore a silly hat,
And danced with a hungry, cheeky cat.
Whispers linger in cracks and seams,
Of mischief, fun, and broken dreams.

As memories fade like sunlight's gleam,
These half-spun tales weave through a dream.
So grab a friend, unlock the past,
And share a giggle that's sure to last.

The Lightness of Being Incomplete

A puzzle missing just one piece,
It laughs and twirls, seeking release.
Though edges rough and colors scant,
It still can dance, and oh, it can't.

With every gap, a chance to play,
It wiggles smiles along the way.
For flaws add flavor, life's sweet spice,
In every bobble, there's a slice.

A half-baked cookie in the tin,
With dough that's soft and lacking skin.
Yet sweetness spills with every bite,
And leaves behind a soft delight.

So let them giggle at the seams,
Those crooked dreams and tangled beams.
For in the dance of twist and turn,
The beauty shines for which we yearn.

Secrets Abound in Quiet Corners

In dusty nooks, where whispers cling,
Secrets hide and shadows sing.
A timid sock, lost in time's weave,
Holds all the stories it can conceive.

A crumb from a feast long-past,
Still holds the flavor, sweet and vast.
It chuckles softly with every tick,
Of clocks that think they're playing tricks.

Light slips through cracks where dust bunnies roam,
Echoing laughter that calls you home.
Each creak of the floorboards shares a plot,
With tales of mischief, it's never forgot.

So peek inside where secrets lay,
And let the past dance in the fray.
For in the quiet, fun can unfold,
With just a hint of stories untold.

Footprints of the Unseen

In the corner a sock has fled,
Hiding out with crumbs instead.
A shoe without its pair so grim,
Where'd you go? It's on a whim!

Keys once jingled, now reside,
Under cushions, where dust bunnies hide.
A map to nowhere, it seems to be,
Where's the last place I had my glee?

Laughter echoes in empty halls,
When I trip over invisible walls.
Mysteries of missing objects sway,
Who knew a broom could dance today?

So I cherish moments so absurd,
A tale of mischief, yet unheard.
In this chaos, a smile will bloom,
As I search the depths of my own room.

Glances at the Unwritten

Oh, the coffee cup, now a mystery,
Once claimed my attention, now lost history.
The mug has taken a vacation,
To realms of delightful imagination.

The fridge whispers secrets, cold and bold,
While countdowns for dinners begin to unfold.
Each empty shelf speaks of meals we've missed,
In this comedy of food, I can't resist.

Chairs that wobble, while laughter sings,
They tell of secrets and playful springs.
In the blink of an eye, I lose the plot,
What was I cooking? Oh, it's all gone to rot!

With every glance, a story appears,
A jest of reality that tickles our fears.
In forgotten corners, joy will persist,
As I try to remember what I'm meant to list.

The Joyful Journey of Wayward Things

A sandwich left, in the backpack's dark abyss,
Its journey begun, led to an unknown bliss.
Doodles and papers clutter around,
What tales they tell, in silence profound.

Lost remote on a treacherous quest,
Sought for channel-surfing, it surely knew best.
The cat lounges, like a ruler supreme,
While I wanders in this absurd dream.

Every corner hides a laugh or two,
At the mischief sparked when tidying up, who knew?
Through tangled wires, bright stories emerge,
Celebrating the goofy, where we all surge.

In this circus of chaos, let's toast to the night,
To keys that won't come back and socks that just might.
In our hearts, the memories will cling,
As we dance through the mischief of everyday fling.

Threads of Humor Woven in Time

A shoelace dances, trips over air,
While mismatched socks twirl without a care.
Falling into laughter, there's a cheer,
Who knew that the laundry could bring such a seer?

The calendar flips to days unplanned,
Where chaos reigns and we understand.
Ticklish days, chasing shadows away,
Where giggles replace what we couldn't say.

Old recipes hide in a pot full of dreams,
Stewing in possibilities, bursting at the seams.
A pinch of absurd, a sprinkle of spice,
Cooking up moments that feel oh-so-nice.

Threads weave in laughter as we recall,
Colors of joy in the fabric of all.
In this tapestry spun with delight,
Every stitch reminds us of the light.

A Locket Full of Memories

In pockets deep, the treasures hide,
The jingle of coins, joy's wild ride.
Each little charm, a story told,
Of spilled drinks, and nights bold.

A shoe on the roof, a hat in the tree,
What a mess, but oh, so free!
Chasing lost items, we laugh and scuffle,
With every misstep, a little more shuffle.

The crumbs we leave, a trail of cheer,
In every corner, forgotten beer.
Misplaced but treasured, like yesterday's song,
Making the moments all the more strong.

Collecting our blunders, those whimsical finds,
Jogging our memories, twisting our minds.
In the locket of life, we'll humorously see,
The keys that unlock our memory spree.

Laughter at the Edge of Forgetting

Tick-tock goes the clock, but I can't find my phone,
Searching high and low, feeling so alone.
In the fridge once again, I forgot my drink,
Oh the giggles rise, before I can think.

Collecting odd socks, a cap and a shoe,
Half of a sandwich, a mystery too.
With each absent object, I burst out in glee,
For every lost thing, there's a new tale for me.

The dog stole the keys, what a ridiculous game!
Chasing him down, but this seems rather lame.
In the end, we all laugh, rolling on the floor,
For every misstep just opens new doors.

With a giggle and grin, I make each mistake,
Counting the gaps, for giggles' own sake.
The edge of forgetting holds laughter so bright,
As we dance through the chaos, under the light.

Unlocking the Door to Today

Ring-ring goes the bell, but I forgot my key,
Locked out of adventure, what a sight to see!
With a wink and a laugh, I knock on the wall,
Hand on my hip, I'm having a ball.

Jumbling my thoughts like my car keys in tow,
Each day a puzzle, where did they go?
Floating on whims, like a balloon up high,
Searching my pockets, wishing to fly.

The kettle's a-howlin', the toast isn't set,
But I'm chuckling to myself, no need for upset.
For every missed moment, there's joy to be found,
In laughter and antics, our hearts stay unbound.

So here's to today, in each mishap or glee,
To the keys that we fumble, reminding us to be free.
Unlocking the moments, with humor we sway,
In the dance of existence, we'll laugh all the way.

The Puzzles We Leave Behind

A puzzle exists in every day's twist,
Like a sock that wanders, into the mist.
With giggles and chuckles, we jest and we play,
For the lost little things show us the way.

The keys on the counter, the phone in the fridge,
What a fine mess, like a runaway bridge.
In search of the things that take our time,
With laughter as currency, all feels like a rhyme.

Each little chaos, an adventure unfolds,
A tale of mishaps, like treasures of gold.
For in every blunder, the glimmers align,
Revealing the love that makes life truly shine.

So let's cherish the laughter, the silliness found,
In the spaces between, where the joy is unbound.
The pieces we scatter, like breadcrumbs in tow,
Craft the puzzles of memories, helping us grow.

Jokes Left Hanging in the Air

Why did the chicken cross the road?
To dodge a pun and break the code!
A punchline missed, oh what a tease,
   Now it's lost among the leaves.

Knock-knock jokes without a door,
Just echoes bouncing on the floor.
A giggle trapped in a sneeze,
   Turns curiosity to a wheeze.

Why was the broom late to the show?
Because it swept too low to know!
The laughter lags behind the scenes,
   As we search for playful means.

A rubber chicken starts to dance,
It juggles puns at every chance.
Each silly tale a twist and twirl,
   A comedy in a chaotic whirl.

A Pondering of Whims

In a world of fancies, what to choose?
A hat that spins or shoes that snooze?
Mismatched socks with stripes and spots,
Make me giggle and connect the dots.

A cat that meows in riddles and rhymes,
Or a dog that fetches the lost times?
Whimsical thoughts float around my head,
While I wonder where my fork has fled.

Chasing shadows of playful dreams,
Like ice cream sodas with fizzy beams.
Every quirky thought takes flight,
In a bubble bath of sheer delight.

With cookies crumbling on the floor,
And giggles waiting behind the door.
Pondering whims that dance like bees,
In a garden of mischievous ease.

Echoes That Weren't Meant to Fade

A rubber band that snaps and sings,
Echoing truths of silly flings.
Whispers of laughter rush and flee,
While dancing shadows climb a tree.

Forgotten pranks beneath the bed,
The noise of giggles left unsaid.
In the attic, a jester's hat,
Echoes of joy where the laughter sat.

A whoopee cushion tells its tale,
While sock puppets stumble and fail.
Every chuckle, a fleeting trace,
In a game of hide-and-seek, we race.

Voices mingle in a playful shout,
The echoes linger all about.
Memories stitched in colors bright,
A tapestry of whimsy and light.

The Quirkiness of Closed Doors

A doorbell that sings off-key,
As if it's nervous to agree.
Behind the panel, jokes await,
With secret smiles and giggles straight.

The doorknob twists in merry glee,
Cracking jokes with each turn I see.
But when I knock, it just retreats,
Playing hide and seek with treats.

A closet spills out hats galore,
Each one a character to explore.
With musty coats that sway and spin,
Silly encounters in wardrobes begin.

A door with hinges squeaks a tune,
While socks escape like a mad raccoon.
With every entrance, new delights,
The quirky magic of moonlit nights.

The Unscripted Adventures of Hidden Effervescence

In a world of socks that disappear,
Each step a puzzle, what's the score?
With giggles tucked in between the seams,
We chase our shadows, laughing more.

Invisible capers under the sun,
A dance of chaos, all in play,
Find me stumbling, tripping on fun,
As nimble dreams flutter away.

A sandwich splattered, oh what a sight,
Mayo rivulets down someone's shirt,
We crack up loudly, no need for fright,
When laughter spreads, oh how we flirt.

Inside the drawers of forgotten things,
A symphony of misfit toys,
The jester's grin, the joy it brings,
In these odd trinkets, we find our joys.

Radiant Reflections in Mundane Moments

On a Tuesday, the sun just peeks,
Coffee spills like laughter's grace,
With mismatched socks and playful tweaks,
In every fumble, there's a trace.

A shoe misplaced on the run,
Yet, my cat claims it as her throne,
Dancing through chores, oh what fun,
Finding joy where seeds are sown.

Sunshine sneaks through window cracks,
Birds chirp, their tweets a silly tune,
In daily drudgery, humor lacks,
Yet here we smile, the afternoon.

A crusty biscuit, half a roll,
It rolls away, a funny chase,
Life's little quirks, they touch the soul,
A hearty laugh ends every race.

The Keyring of Wistful Tidings

Tangled keys on a ring of fate,
Jingling stories of times mislaid,
Unlocking laughter, hearts elate,
Every jingle, a quest portrayed.

The doorbell rings; a friend appears,
With a hat too big and mismatched shoes,
We laugh at folly, shed our fears,
In every slip, there's joy to choose.

A treasure map drawn in crayon bold,
Leads us to where the ice cream stands,
In melted strokes, adventures told,
Life's simple pleasures in sticky hands.

Sparking moments caught on film,
With goofy grins and peace signs flashed,
In life's gallery, laughter's hymn,
In every snapshot, memories crashed.

Whimsy Wrapped in the Ordinary

In the kitchen, a spatula flies,
Pancakes flip like clouds at dawn,
With a splash and a squeak of surprise,
Breakfast battles, the day's new song.

Plants dressed in dusty old hats,
Dance gracefully in breezy cheer,
Among the pots, where daydreams chat,
Whispers of nature, sweet and clear.

By the mailbox, a letter sings,
No postage paid; the joy was free,
Within the words, a tale that clings,
Wrapped up in chuckles, just like me.

A squirrel steals lunch, a playful thief,
Chasing it down, we burst with glee,
In the mundane, find laughter's reef,
In the quirks of day, we dance carefree.

The Hidden Treasures of Joyful Misadventures

In chaos, we often find
Little gems of a silly kind.
With laughter echoing in the air,
We trip and tumble without a care.

Mismatched socks and tangled hair,
Dance with joy, a carefree pair.
Around the corner, mishaps greet,
Each stumble brings a funny beat.

Lost in thought while chasing a dream,
With every turn, there's a comical theme.
Unexpected twists weave our fate,
Embracing the silly, never too late.

So here's to the moments we create,
Where humor finds us, it's never late.
Life's funny quirks, a priceless delight,
Hidden treasures in every night.

Chasing Shadows of Playful Remembrance

In dim-lit halls where shadows play,
We chase the giggles of yesterday.
A whispered joke in the fading light,
Turns the mundane into pure delight.

Forgotten toys under the bed,
Awaken memories that dance in our head.
Jumping high as a fleeting dream,
In the golden glow, we're a joyous team.

A wobbly chair becomes a throne,
In this realm where silliness is grown.
We toss confetti on faded sighs,
Together we laugh as the past flies by.

With echoes of fun in every nook,
We turn the pages of our storybook.
From silly trips to moments sublime,
Chasing shadows is truly divine.

Fragments of Glee Beneath the Couch

Beneath the couch, what do we find?
Lost treasures of a jester's mind.
Coins of laughter, crumbs of cheer,
The little joys that we hold dear.

Dust bunnies twirl in a playful dance,
As we dive in for a funny chance.
A rubber chicken, mismatched keys,
A forgotten joke, a gentle tease.

We sift through moments, both big and small,
In our quest for humor, we discover all.
Each piece we unearth brings a hearty grin,
Reminding us that joy lies within.

So if you feel a bit off track,
Look beneath the couch, there's no lack.
With each fragment, a giggle may bloom,
In the treasure trove of our living room.

Serendipity's Dance in Distant Hallways

In the twist of fate, we often trip,
On a hidden joke or a playful quip.
Each corner turned, a surprise awaits,
With giggles igniting the mundane states.

Distant hallways echo with charm,
Where laughter dances, unarmed.
A silly tune that makes us sway,
Brings sunshine on a gloomy day.

Sometimes we stumble, and oh, we grin,
For every mishap, there's joy to win.
In the flurry of chance, we twirl about,
Embracing the laughter that's all around.

So let us wander through life's ballet,
Where serendipity leads the way.
In distant hallways, together we laugh,
Crafting memories, a delightful craft.

Secrets Stored in Dust

In corners of my home, they hide,
Old treasures gone, the time has lied.
A dusty shoe, a book of yore,
Whispers secrets, tales of more.

A sippy cup with milk still in,
Stuck beneath the chair's own skin.
Old socks that dance, and mice that play,
In the shadows, they laugh away.

Underneath the pile of clothes,
Are long-lost friends, where nobody goes.
With every tug, a giggle springs,
For life's bizarre, and oh, it sings!

Unraveled yarn and crumpled dreams,
In this clutter, joy redeems.
With every dust bunny that hops,
A chuckle sprouts, and never stops.

The Adventure of Missing Gems

Once upon a time, I swore,
The cat had gems upon the floor.
With every leap and every bound,
They seemed to vanish without a sound.

A shiny spoon, my favorite fork,
Resided with the missing cork.
Searching high, searching low,
In drawers, cupboards, don't you know?

An epic hunt for sparkly things,
Led me to a box of strings.
I laughed aloud, what a grand prize,
Just knots and threads before my eyes!

Yet in this quest, my heart was light,
For in the chaos, pure delight.
With giggles chasing, I would roam,
In a world of wonders, I felt at home.

When Chuckles Echo Down the Hall

In halls so wide, with echoes clear,
Footsteps dance, yet no one's near.
A ticklish ghost in fluffy shoes,
Creeps along with silly news.

Around the bend, a laugh would chase,
The curtains swayed, a jolly race.
Mirrors wink and pictures smirk,
Every shadow starts to jerk.

The bumps and thuds ignite the night,
Turning whispers into fright.
Though shadows play, and ghosts might tease,
I find a chuckle with such ease.

So hear the giggles as they soar,
With every creak, I start to roar.
In haunted halls, I find my thrill,
Laughter echoes, bending will!

The Art of Misplaced Grins

In pockets deep, my frown a charm,
It led me straight to mischief's farm.
With grins that glow, I seek the jest,
Yet misplaced smiles refuse to rest.

A bag of tricks, the jester's plight,
Wobbly chairs that bring delight.
A flailing arm, a splatter of pie,
As laughter blooms, I barely fly.

Upon the stage, I've lost my cue,
Yet with the crowd, I find what's true.
Twists and turns, the dance of glee,
In every oops, there's joy to see.

So gather 'round, my merry folk,
Together we'll weave the richest joke.
For in this world, so mixed and spun,
The art of joy has just begun!

The Dance of Hidden Treasures

In corners dark, gems do hide,
The jester laughs, with keys inside.
They twirl and spin, in playful glee,
Unlocking doors to mystery.

A sock and spoon, they caper too,
Joined by a cup that once was blue.
With every jingle, hearts ignite,
As treasures dive into the night.

Behind the couch, a world awaits,
Of playful launches and funny fates.
Each forgotten bit, a tale to weave,
In a space where jesters believe.

So wander forth, let laughter soar,
And dance with things you can't ignore.
For every lost, there's something found,
In playful moments, joy unbound.

Tales from a Forgotten Drawer

A drawer creeped slow, a gentle sigh,
Inside the chaos, dreams fly by.
A lone button chuckles with delight,
While pens and papers join the fight.

There's a ticket stub from days of yore,
A matchbook from that pizza store.
They banter back, recount their fun,
Under the watch of a crumpled pun.

Old chewing gum, a time ago,
Giggles echo, memories flow.
With every peek and shuffled mess,
A chuckle finds, and joy's caress.

So when you stumble on treasure old,
Rekindle the stories, let them bolder.
For in forgotten things, we see,
The joy it brings, a jubilee.

Mirage of Unfulfilled Adventures

Once a map that led to gold,
A rogue was lost, or so I'm told.
In laughter, find the twists and bends,
As misfits gather, plotting ends.

Each path they took, a silly chase,
With every slip, they'd win the race.
A crowing rooster starts the fun,
As laughter echoes, dreams begun.

The compass spins, a dizzy dance,
As folktales weave a merry chance.
For every twist and turn they roam,
Is but a quest, the heart's true home.

So chase the visions, wild and free,
With each misstep, find harmony.
In golden dreams, together we weave,
The mirage blooms, if you believe.

The Serendipity of Misplaced Things

Oh, where's my phone? A duckling cries,
Like magic tricks, they slip and slide.
A cat just yawns, a sly awake,
While shoes take off, for fun's own sake.

A glance beneath a mountain small,
Reveals an apple, round and tall.
In laughter's grip, we find our way,
Through jumbles bright, we dance and play.

Keys to nowhere, but oh so fun,
Their laughter twinkles, just begun.
While clocks tick on, in secret rhyme,
They waltz through pockets, lost in time.

So when you're stuck, don't fret or grieve,
Smile and dance, and just believe.
For in the chaos, joys do ring,
In misplaced things, the heart takes wing.

Revelry Along the Forgotten Path

Amidst the trees, we prance and roam,
With pockets jingling, like a gnome.
A bird laughs loud, a squirrel does twist,
We start a dance, none can resist.

The sun peeks through, giggles abound,
With every step, new joys are found.
But wait! What's that? A shoe, a hat,
We end up tangled; a comical spat.

Winding trails of jests and cheer,
We skip and hop from here to there.
Who needs a map? Who needs a plan?
Just follow laughter, if you can!

So take the road paved with delight,
Where every shadow sparks a light.
In a world of jest, we're never lost,
Collecting smiles, no matter the cost.

Unhinging Laughter in Silent Spaces

In quiet corners, mischief brews,
A whispered joke, a winking muse.
The clock strikes two, a chuckle fades,
As sudden giggles launch cascades.

Beneath the stairs, a puppy's yawn,
Turns into laughter at the dawn.
We trip on thoughts, our minds collide,
In every mishap, joy won't hide.

Chasing whispers through the hall,
A duster sweeps, off goes the wall!
With paint now gone, we stare in glee,
At this wild art of liberty.

So join the fun, don't hold your breath,
In silly games, we flirt with death.
For every blunder, oh what a thrill!
We find our treasures, as we will!

Chronicles of Chuckles and Wandering Hearts

Through valleys low, on hills so steep,
We gather tales we wish to keep.
In every step, a laugh, a fumble,
With each misstep, our hearts do tumble.

The moonlit night ignites a quest,
Where shadows dance and jesters jest.
A muffin thrown, a pie a-splatter,
These things we'll remember, oh, what matter!

With every giggle, roads unwind,
A friendly bicker, mirth designed.
As freedom calls in nightly air,
We roam, we jest, with not a care.

And when the dawn begins to creep,
We've chased our dreams, we've danced, we leap.
In every memory, we find our song,
The tales of us, where we belong!

Forgotten Riddles in the Midst of Play

In tangled grass, we hide and seek,
Where whispers echo, learn to speak.
A riddle tossed on playful breeze,
Unlocks the secrets with such ease.

We spin in circles, giggled tight,
A world of whimsy, pure delight.
Our shoes untied, our hair a mess,
Each stumble fuels our happiness.

A game of tag leads us astray,
With buzzing laughter here to stay.
If just a sock sparks merry chats,
We'll trade our woes for friendly spats.

So leap and bound, the day is young,
With silly stories yet unsung.
In every riddle, in every glee,
We find the keys to what's carefree.

Whispers of Joy in Forgotten Corners

In the drawer of time, we search and fumble,
A sock with a hole and a toy that can tumble.
Laughter rings out like a bell on the wall,
As memories dance in a twinkling sprawl.

Beneath old newspapers, we shove and we pry,
A penny, a button, a note with a sigh.
The joy in the hunt, though chaos it brings,
We chuckle and grin as the treasure it sings.

With an old dusty lamp and a dream from the past,
We find silly things that were meant to last.
A charm that once sparkled in someone's eye,
Now tucked in a corner where secrets lie.

In every forgotten nook where we peek,
We find little wonders, a moment unique.
So here's to the hunt, with its quirks and its cheer,
For laughter is magic that echoes so clear.

The Echoes of Cheerful Wandering

Through winding lanes where shadows play,
We stumble and giggle along the pathway.
A hat on a pigeon, a dance in the rain,
The joy of the silly makes time feel inane.

With coffee in hand and a grin on our face,
We find sparkles of humor in every place.
A skater who tumbles, a baby who squeals,
These moments are gems that true joy reveals.

The wind carries whispers of jokes yet untold,
Unraveling laughter like threads made of gold.
An umbrella that flips, a balloon on the breeze,
These quirky encounters bring hearts to their knees.

And when we return, full of tales to share,
The stories of wanderings lift spirits in air.
For joy finds a way when we wander with glee,
In echoes of laughter, we're ever so free.

Unlocking the Secrets of Fleeting Moments

With keys of imagination, we unlock the day,
Where squirrels in hats find the best place to play.
A blink of an eye and a wink from the cat,
Turns mundane to magic, imagine that!

The clock ticks away, but we dance in the sun,
Chasing butterflies, each moment a fun run.
Oh, spark of a joke, oh, glint of surprise,
As laughter erupts like bright fireworks in skies.

At the corner café, where all stories blend,
We sip on our drinks, as old friends we mend.
With crumbs on our shirts and giggles that flow,
The joy in our hearts gives the world a sweet glow.

Unlocking the secrets that time tries to hide,
We revel in chuckles, not too far to glide.
For laughter is golden, a moment's true art,
A treasure we hold in the depths of our heart.

A Symphony of Smiles in Everyday Journeys

Underneath the umbrella, where puddles collide,
We splash past the raindrops; our laughter's the guide.
Every footstep a beat in this whimsical tune,
A cab driver's quip brings the sun out at noon.

In lines at the store, where boredom could loom,
A toddler's wild dance fills the air with a boom.
With winks and good cheer, we make time stand still,
Creating a symphony, whose notes give us thrill.

As we travel through lanes lined with wonders anew,
Each moment unravels something silly to view.
A cat on a leash with a jogger in tow,
Bringing smiles to our faces like confetti from snow.

And at day's gentle close, as the shadows grow long,
We share in our stories, a bright joyful song.
For every small moment, we find in the fray,
It's a dance full of giggles along the way.

Lost Trinkets in a World of Grins

Tiny baubles playing hide and seek,
Under cushions, a shy little peek.
Jingling coins with a secret to share,
Giggles echo in the clumsy air.

Forgotten pebbles, memories float,
In pockets deep, they wiggle and gloat.
Adventures start with a flick of a wrist,
Chasing shadows, you get the gist.

A button rolls in a dance so spry,
While socks unite in a wild, bold try.
Chasing whims like playful sprites,
Silly moments, heart's delight.

With each lost trinket, a tale unwinds,
Whimsical fables that fate entwines.
So let's embrace the chaotic spree,
For treasures found are wild and free.

The Soundtrack of Unseen Moments

Bouncing marbles and laughter's jingle,
Echoing memories as giggles mingle.
A serenade of whoops and slips,
When life takes a tumble, we share the quips.

In kitchens bright, spoons start to dance,
Spicy aromas join in the prance.
Forgotten rhythms, a tune akin,
Joy bursts forth with every grin.

Ghostly whispers from a jar of mints,
Tickle our minds as we catch the hints.
Chasing shadows of playful cheer,
The tune of the everyday we hold dear.

Roaring laughter on a sunlit day,
Synchronized sillies come out to play.
With every chuckle, a note to compose,
A symphony of joy, in which we chose.

Jests and Journeys Beyond the Doorstep

With a skip and a hop, adventures begin,
Off we go, with a cheeky grin.
To unseen places, through laughter's gate,
Where mischief awaits, oh, isn't it great?

Each little mishap, a ticket to glee,
Fumbling footsteps, as grand as can be.
A dance with fate on a winding lane,
Turning chaos into laughter's gain.

Puppies darting, through puddles they splash,
Chasing the sunlight, a joyous clash.
Every twist brings a silly surprise,
With each crooked step, we soar to the skies.

A pair of socks, wearing mismatched flair,
Guide us onward, with jocular air.
So let's wander where folly presides,
In the realm of jest, true fun abides.

The Mysterious Quest for Absent Accessories

A search for spectacles, they lie in disguise,
Hiding in corners with mischievous sighs.
With every turn, a chuckle we find,
As the missing piece plays tricks on the mind.

Keys dancing proudly, then slipping away,
Scattering laughter throughout the fray.
Puzzle pieces in a whimsical race,
A chase ensues, full of merry face.

Brooches and bangles, where have they fled?
In the realm of chaos, they merrily tread.
A sock and a shoe soon join the parade,
Each wayward wanderer jokes that we made.

Finally we find what was sought all along,
When the funniest stories come bursting in song.
In every lost item, a giggle resides,
As we laugh through the treasures that fate provides.

The Jingle of Abandoned Dreams

In a pocket, they chime, those wishes once bright,
Forgotten in corners, lost out of sight.
They dance with old coins, a shuffle of cheer,
Whispering secrets that tickle the ear.

With laughter, they mingle through shadows and light,
A melody sweet, a humorous flight.
Each jingling token, a story it tells,
Of moments once held, now in jumbled spells.

In the chaos of change, we trip on our glee,
Stumbling on echoes, just let it be free.
For life's little treasures, though misplaced at times,
Will shift in our pockets, making us rhyme.

So gather your trinkets, your whimsical fate,
Embrace all the laughter; it's never too late.
With bells that still jingle, they beckon the fun,
Old dreams may have faded, but joy's just begun.

Unlocking the Joy Within

In a drawer full of nonsense, I find a bright key,
Not for doors, but for smiles set loose and carefree.
It jangles and wiggles, a joy to behold,
Cracking up the moments, worth more than gold.

Let's tumble through troubles with giggles galore,
As the key turns in laughter, we open the door.
To a room full of memories, silly and grand,
Where the sunshine of jest holds a playful hand.

The locks that once bothered now rust in their fate,
For humor unlocks what we deem as too late.
So twist that old knob, let the chuckles fly high,
And watch as the worries drift up to the sky.

For every lost item just hides a good joke,
Behind every treasure, a tickle it stokes.
So laugh through the chaos, it's the key to the bliss,
Unlocking the wonders we'd almost dismissed.

Echoes of Mirthful Moments

In a room where the shadows sneak quietly,
Lies laughter's old echo, as joyful as can be.
It bounces off walls, boisterous and bright,
A symphony of giggles filling up the night.

Each chuckle a ripple, each snicker a song,
In the embrace of the silly, we always belong.
Just turn up the volume, let folly resound,
For in those wild echoes, our spirits are found.

Though keys may be absent, all things can be found,
In the heart of the laughter, love's always around.
So dance to the rhythm of absurdity's beat,
And wear the crown of whimsy, life's joyous treat.

With every shared moment, let mirth take its flight,
In this whimsical echo, all worries take flight.
Revel in the sounds of delightful refrain,
For the joy of the present eclipses the pain.

The Curious Case of Missing Trinkets

Oh, the mysteries dwell where my knickknacks have fled,

A puzzle of items, where's that old thread?
A button, a cap, lost under the couch,
Missing in action, like a magical slouch.

The quest for the quirky, that mug with a grin,
Takes me on journeys through thick and through thin.
With each silly find, giggles bubble and burst,
Turning mundane moments into whimsical firsts.

I check all my pockets, my shoes and my hat,
Giggling at memories of where I've been at.
As laughter reveals all, the treasures appear,
In the corners of chaos, oh, how they adhere!

For in every lost item, a chuckle resides,
A wink from the universe, where silliness guides.
So celebrate trinkets, both hidden and found,
In the curious case where joy's tightly wound.

Twists of Fate and Fumbling Hands

In the kitchen, a spoon takes flight,
Out the window, in a silly fright.
Chasing after a wayward fork,
Life feels like a comical cork.

Each morning brings a new surprise,
Like mismatched socks and lopsided ties.
With every mishap, a chuckle born,
As tangled thoughts like ribbons are worn.

The dog steals a sandwich in a dash,
While the cat makes a monumental crash.
Fingers slip while aiming for bread,
Oh, how we laugh at the chaos ahead!

Through clumsy trips and fumbling tries,
We find our joy in goofy sighs.
So raise a toast to blunders sweet,
For every stumble, a twist that's neat.

Echoes of Guffaws in the Attic

In the attic, dust bunnies dance,
Hiding secrets with each glance.
A rubber chicken falls with a thump,
Making the old trunks giggle and jump.

Forgotten toys mirror old delight,
Jokes linger here, woven tight.
Underneath layers of cobwebs spun,
Laughter finds a way to run.

An umbrella pops open, sudden surprise,
Tickling laughter, we can't disguise.
With echoes ringing from walls so tall,
Every corner awaits a comical call.

Memories wrapped in riddles untold,
Where mischief and humor are bold.
In the attic's embrace, we find our spark,
As giggles flutter like whispers in the dark.

The Mirthful Art of Letting Go

A juggler's ball rolls under the chair,
We watch it bounce with delighted flair.
As clumsy fingers slip and swerve,
We drop our worries, it's time to serve!

Embrace the slips, the trips, the spills,
Like ice cream cones and sunshine thrills.
With every laugh, a burden lifts,
Joy awaits in playful gifts.

Dancing shadows on the grassy lawn,
Chasing dreams until the dawn.
In wild abandon, we twirl and spin,
Letting go of troubles buried within.

The world can wait, we've time to play,
In bright absurdity, we'll find our way.
From little blunders, big grins grow,
The art of laughter in the flow.

Keyholes and Dreamcatchers

A key turns in the mailbox door,
But only love letters and nothing more.
With every twist, a tale unfolds,
Misplaced treasures, the heart upholds.

Dreamcatchers sway with stories untold,
We catch our giggles, let them unfold.
Each wish tied with a yarn of bright hue,
Catching mischief, like sticky glue.

The key to laughter is easily found,
Among squeaky floors and playful sound.
A lost shoe here, a misplaced hat,
Turn around; can you find that cat?

Unlock the moments that make you smile,
Through whimsy and folly, we wander a mile.
In keyholes and dreams, our spirits roam,
For joy is the treasure we call our home.

Moments Snatched from Oblivion

In the kitchen, the spoon dances,
The cat steals a glance as it prances.
Forgotten dinners, we just can't recall,
Yet laughter erupts; we savor it all.

Chasing our thoughts like a mischievous breeze,
Stumbling on hiccups, we drop to our knees.
A sock in the fridge, a hat on the floor,
These snippets of chaos, we can't help but adore.

Napping on couches, a glow from the screen,
Mismatched the socks, oh, what does it mean?
We giggle and grin at the puzzle we weave,
In these tiny moments, what more could we need?

With keys on the counter, we scatter and roam,
In absurdity's arms, we find ourselves home.
Serendipity's clasp whispers softly, it seems,
"Stay here, my dear, in these wonderful dreams."

The Sound of a Silent Door

There's a creak in the hallway, a squeak from the chair,
While the world buzzes by without worry or care.
A child's yellow notebook—oh, what did it say?
With doodles and scribbles, it brightens the day.

As the clock ticks in rhythm, a joke comes alive,
With a wink and a nod, the old fridge will chive.
We roll on the carpet, hearts light as a feather,
A chorus of giggles, we're light as the weather.

When the door swings wide with a plop and a thud,
We trip over shoes, oh, what a fine flood!
The hustle of moments all rush through the air,
In the mess of it all, we find moments to share.

A bell rings next door; oh, what could it be?
A party, a dance, just to feel oh so free.
The sound of the laughter spills out on the street,
With hearts all a-flutter, we can't miss the beat.

Whimsical Trails of the Unseen

In the park, a balloon floats away in delight,
With kids chasing dreams on their scooters so bright.
But oh look, a dog, with a shoe in its grip,
A silly parade, what a comical trip!

A trail of confetti, like magic it swirls,
A gathering of giggles, both boys and their curls.
Somewhere, there's ice cream with sprinkles galore,
Yet someone's lost count of just how many more!

Laughter echoes wildly, a melody shared,
With flip-flops on feet that are slightly impaired.
The ice cream drips down—oh, what a sweet mess!
Yet smiles never fade; they're a soft, warm caress.

Each moment a lesson wrapped up in a cheer,
As we wander through chaos, we hold it all dear.
The beauty of moments that swirl through the sun,
In whimsical trails, we've all just begun!

The Treasure Map of Everyday Joys

A napkin's a map where the crumbs congregate,
As we search for the treats hiding under the plate.
The coffee pot whistles, it sings with a tune,
While socks form a treasure map under the moon.

With giggles as markings, we outline our quest,
In the garden of goofiness, we're feeling our best.
The sunspots are guides on this mystical path,
Where laughter and kindness share a warm bath.

The keys in the drawer, oh where could they be?
Not a worry at all, we've got plenty of glee.
With wild imagination, we sail on a breeze,
Discovering treasures, with playful degrees.

Each day a new riddle, each night a new prize,
In the chaos of moments, we see through our eyes.
With friends by our side, every heartache, a ploy,
In this map of existence, we find endless joy!

Seeking Spirits in the Shadows

In corners sneaky and dark,
Dwell whispers that tease and spark.
With giggles hidden in gloom,
We dance in the cluttered room.

A sock with a tale to share,
Floats past with an airy flair.
Chasing echoes, we trip and fall,
On laughter painted on the wall.

The cat, with a twitch of tail,
Claims victory where we would fail.
As shadows prance around the floor,
They join our mischief evermore.

We seek the lost, yet find the fun,
In a world where we never shun.
Spirits wink from behind the chair,
As we chuckle and banter without a care.

The Jangle of Unseen Connections

A keychain jingles, oh what a show,
With charms that mimic life's ebb and flow.
Each jangle whispers tales of yore,
Of nights spent searching, adventures galore.

A puzzle piece here, scattered dreams,
In springs of laughter, nothing's as it seems.
We lose our grip but regain our cheer,
With every folly, we hold dear.

The fridge hums a tune we all know,
As we gather around, spirits aglow.
In every stumble, the universe winks,
Pulling together what no one thinks.

Connections spark in shades of fun,
In the search for keys, two hearts spun.
An unseen bond in a cluttered mess,
Brings joy that we absolutely bless.

Fables of Forgotten Clusters

In the attic of memories, dust collects,
Where stories huddle like playful suspects.
Boxes stacked high with bits of old bits,
Breathing tales of laughter and fits.

A rogue pair of shoes, a tale untold,
Whispers of mischief in glitter and gold.
Each cluster forgets what shouldn't be lost,
Yet finds the warm moments, despite the cost.

The mirror winks, reflecting the past,
As we tumble through fables, unsurpassed.
With every stumble, we giggle aloud,
Crafting legends that make us proud.

In corners where laughter seeds grow wide,
Forgotten treasures we won't let slide.
Clusters of joy in the mess all around,
Create a symphony of silliness found.

A Touch of Serendipity

Under cushions where secrets abide,
Lies a treasure, forgotten but wide.
With laughter brightening the shaded floor,
We stumble on smiles we can't ignore.

A banana peel, oh what a sight,
Leads to a fall in a whirlwind of light.
In chaos we see that fate plays a hand,
Turning mishaps into a dance so grand.

Between the cracks of the sidewalk we tread,
Dreams of a moment where laughter is bred.
Chasing moments that slip through our grasp,
We find joy in the humor and gasp.

A touch of whimsy, a nudge from the stars,
In the ordinary, we unravel the jars.
Each twist and turn, a giggle, a chance,
Brings a sprinkle of joy in our merry dance.

Where Laughter Meets Lost Time

In a world where socks go missing,
Tickles hide behind a door.
We chase our tails, no time for hissing,
While giggles echo, we ask for more.

A spoon might turn into a fiddle,
The cat is wearing a shoe.
As we dance around the riddle,
Joy lingers like morning dew.

Minutes slip through our fingers,
Like bubbles in a wacky game.
Here and there, laughter lingers,
While time forgets its name.

In this circus we all belong,
With tricks that never cease.
Clumsy moves and silly songs,
In chaos, we find our peace.

Secrets Beneath the Floorboards

Underneath the creaky tile,
Where whispers hold their breath.
The broom lies down to rest a while,
Hiding secrets of the pest.

A dropped spoon and missing sock,
They tell their tales at night.
Under beds, in every nook,
They waltz in secret light.

Monsters dwell with giggles grand,
As the clock ticks slow.
In a land of dust, we'll make our stand,
Trading woes for the glow.

So when things seem out of place,
With smiles that never quit,
Just look beneath the wooden space,
And find the magic kit.

The Mischief of Wandering Hearts

Hearts that skip like painted stones,
   They tumble, bounce, and play.
With laughter loud, they find their homes,
   In pockets where they stray.

Chasing dreams with silly glee,
   They march like ants in rows.
Through mazes made of whimsy spree,
   Where mischief often grows.

They prance beneath the pumpkin moon,
   Lost keys keep the beat.
In jitterbugs, we'll be in tune,
   With steps that feel so sweet.

So gather 'round, oh wandering souls,
   Embrace the funny plight.
In the dance of breaking molds,
   Find joy in pure delight.

Chronicles of the Unhinged Door

The door squeaks with tales untold,
Of laughter's wild embrace.
Every creak a moment bold,
With smiles that we can trace.

Some days it swings like a wild dance,
With shoes that never fit.
Every knock a fleeting chance,
To enter mischief's wit.

Peeking through that bent old frame,
We spot the hidden glee.
Behind the hinges, that's the game,
Where we can truly be.

So if you hear that raucous roar,
Don't shy away, explore!
For every laugh unlocks a door,
To silly, evermore.

The Chronicles of Missing Tokens and Lively Tales

In pockets deep, the tokens gleam,
They vanish fast, like some wild dream.
A quest begins, with friends in tow,
Chasing shadows, where do they go?

With every step, we twist and turn,
A jingle here, a lesson learned.
We laugh aloud at the silly chase,
For every giggle, there's a trace.

The coins appear in strange old shoes,
A treasure hunt, we can't refuse.
In hidden drawers and under beds,
The stories spin, with fun that spreads.

We leave no stone unturned, it seems,
In playful dawn and evening dreams.
Oh, what a sport, this wild delight,
Collecting tokens through day and night.

Glimmers of Playfulness in Abandoned Places

In dusty halls where giggles hide,
Once vibrant souls now laugh inside.
An echo faint of joy once bold,
In every crack, a history told.

Rusted swings squeak with old-time cheer,
While shadows dance, the past draws near.
A winding path through weeds they tread,
Each step a story, the lost are fed.

With every twist, the whimsy grows,
As time gives way to playful prose.
Through hidden nooks where laughter sings,
A celebration of forgotten things.

In every corner, a twinkle glows,
With whispers soft where mischief flows.
We find the fun in what was lost,
In joyful moments, we count the cost.

Whispers in the Keyhole

Tiny whispers through the frame,
Unlock the secret, stoke the flame.
A giggle caught in the wooden door,
Hiding treasures, calling for more.

What keys were passed, now out of sight,
Unlock the laughter, day and night.
Through keyholes thin, our fingers crawl,
Grabbing memories, old and tall.

A riddle here, a puzzle there,
We seek the joy and find the rare.
With playful nudges and grins so wide,
Inside each lock, our dreams abide.

So peek inside, the tales unfold,
In every whisper, laughter bold.
A key may bend, but joy won't break,
In every heart, that's the keepsake.

Jests of the Forgotten

Once lost in corners dark and gray,
The jesters hide, but still they play.
With every chuckle from the past,
In shadows deep, their joy amassed.

Cracked mirrors hold their playful glee,
Reflections of what once used to be.
An old hat tips, a shoe takes flight,
The forgotten tricks bring pure delight.

With every step where silence reigns,
A giggle bursts from flaking stains.
The jests we find, in layers thick,
Pull laughter forth, a charming trick.

In dusty rooms, we hear them speak,
The humor lingers, mild and sleek.
We gather round, their tales unfold,
In every jest, pure joy retold.

www.ingramcontent.com/pod-product-compliance
Lightning Source LLC
Chambersburg PA
CBHW051631160426
43209CB00004B/599